Rhyming Riddles

Marjorie Craggs
Illustrated by Patrice Aggs

CAMBRIDGE
UNIVERSITY PRESS

I walk on a tightrope,
I hang on a swing,
I fly through the air
Above the big ring.

What am I?

3

My clothes are jet black
and I have two black cats.
I make magic spells
with spiders and rats.

What am I?

I begin with a "c"
and have very soft fur.
I enjoy eating fish.
I hiss and I purr.   What am I?

7

I have a red cross
and I'm painted white.
All the cars let me pass
when I flash my blue light.   What am I?

9

I live in a land
where icy winds blow.
I have very thick fur,
the colour of snow.

What am I?

When children build me
they have lots of fun,
but I melt away quickly
in the hot sun.

What am I?

I begin with a "d".
I have two webbed feet.
I dip under water
to find food to eat.

What am I?

I'm a wild, furry creature,
I leap, hop and bound.
I live in my burrow
under the ground.   What am I?

I am striped black and white,
with a short, spiky mane.
I live in a herd
on the African plain.

What am I?

I have an eye
but I cannot see.
I'm very sharp.
You can sew with me.   What am I?

I don't build my nest
on the branch of a tree.
I nest on the cliffs,
looking over the sea.

What am I?

Answers to Rhyming Riddles

Pages 2 and 3
an acrobat

Pages 4 and 5
a witch

Pages 6 and 7
a cat

Pages 8 and 9
an ambulance

Pages 10 and 11
a polar bear

Pages 12 and 13
a snowman

Pages 14 and 15
a duck

Pages 16 and 17
a rabbit

Pages 18 and 19
a zebra

Pages 20 and 21
a needle

Pages 22 and 23
a seagull

There are some other things hidden in the pictures. Can you find them?

a clown

a horse

a ghost

a nest

an igloo

a jigsaw

The publishers wish to thank the Cambridge branch of the British Red Cross for their help with the illustration on pages 8 and 9.